Peelin' the Onion

Melva T. L. Smith

Peelin' the Onion

by

Melva T. L. Smith

Kravitz & Sons
INNOVATORS IN PUBLISHING, MARKETING AND ADVERTISING

Kravitz and Sons LLC
204 E Arlington Blvd. Suite B
Greenville, NC 27858

© 2025 Melva T.L. Smith. All rights reserved.

No part of this book may be reproduced, stored in a retrieval system, or transmitted by any means without the written permission of the author.

Published by Kravitz and Sons LLC.

ISBN: 979-8-89639-634-5 (e)
ISBN: 979-8-89639-635-2 (hb)

Library of Congress Control Number: 2026902894

Because of the dynamic nature of the Internet, any web addresses or links contained in this book may have changed since publication and may no longer be valid. The views expressed in this work are solely those of the author and do not necessarily reflect the views of the publisher, and the publisher hereby disclaims any responsibility for them.

DREAM

I'm floating on a cloud
heading toward the moon
my star so bright I can touch it soon

Dream big
Dream small

I won't let no one destroy it at all
I see poachers in my mist
trying to bite my cloud but miss
it's my dream, I'm riding high
and can't no man tear me
down tonight

Dream big
Dream small

There are some who mean well but
whisper cautiously to us all
why, that seed of doubt is enough
to tremble us out of our cloud
but stay strong
ride that cloud
it's your dream
be proud

Dream Big with a smile

Relax

After a long, hard day
You have a way to relax me, comfort me, hold me, and love me
Your arms so strong

You can do no wrong
because I know that
we belong
together

Times may be rough
but I'll never have enough
of you and me

I am for you and you are for me
So just let us be
relax me!

FLICKER

A hush of stillness fills the air, the sound of your match stroking the box to light me

Then nothing, is that all nothing? Nothing else? My life is bright as I flicker for you. Watch me dance with joy. Yes, I'm melting, don't leave, I'm just feeling the things I think I ought to feel.

I'm alone, just melting away, wondering day by day, am I real or just for play? I flicker and dance for you but I'm still alone, praying that someone would ring that phone and join me.

Until then just put me in a window! What…you just snuffed me out, my tears are running down my side, expressing my cold and sad goodbyes.

We Got Soul

Sweet Sixteen, what an age to be
Sweet Sixteen was a great age to me
Like the winds that pass through time
Like the life of your music but with a subtle rhyme
The talk is like none other for the words,
I can tell it's from a sister or brother.
No, it's not a black thang, white thang, female thang, or a male thang,
it's a Radio Soul Thang
The thang that opens our hearts and our minds
To which is given to us at any given time

We Got Soul

You Are

When the sun shines it nurtures our plant life. When it rains if it is too cold it may bring on some pain.

But, when it is a hot day that rain makes it all better, it takes the pain away.

Storms grow near and some storms grow far; no, it never touches that northern star to which **You are**

It's true, my love; They'll never be another us. Some may try but all they end up with is rust.

Waves can be hard and the ocean rough; if you can't stand then that will be the end of us.

For **you are** my strength my beacon of light.

You pulsate like a heart, bring love to my life.

You are my thunder, my lightning, the moon, sun, and stars; but without you I'll lose my way. Life will be dark. For I would have no need for that beacon because I am already DEAD, with no heart beat-n.

AS WE GROW

We are nurtured from the start. All because someone had the heart to show me love. It comes from above and within. That love was given with a subtle grin.

AS WE GROW

So big, so tall, so strong with many arms to hold you; I sprout bearing gifts of beauty and bliss. Defying laws of gravity; breaking the ropes that bind me.

AS WE GROW

People come and go, some appear just to watch me grow. As seasons change I do too. Why does this make parts of me hang, wither, fall, or droop? Is it because I am alone? Is it because life can be cruel? Is it because I'm alone? It's cold.

AS WE GROW

There may be no answers for my questions; that leaves me to think they'll change or go away with the blowing of the wind.

AS WE GROW

Ahhh, it's warm again & there are people everywhere. Do I dare, do I dare; Show my

brilliant color and make them stare. I'm full, thick, and strong again, safe from harm again. OR, am I....

AS WE GROW

TIME IS OF THE ESSENCE

Day to day we find a way to see, to hear and to hold thee.

Time is of the Essence

Through a long day I hear no voice, have no choice but to remain astray.

Time is of the Essence

When I hear Billie's Blues and who knows what to do, I think of you wanting, needing, and yearning.

Time is of the Essence

Although I've tried I really need to say goodbye. It's hard to lose that part of thee. PLEASE, one more time, for me!

Time is of the Essence

Ummmmmm! Yummy!

As the wind blows, sun shines, and grapes turns into vintage wine. There's no one like you that can melt my heart. Taste so sweat! OOOhh, good enough to eat. Your chocolate melts my heart, so pleasing to the tongue. Close my eyes. Do you feel it—OOoooohh, here it comes At any season or any given reason you are always pleasing to the taste of life. There seems to be a chemistry between us, you see!

KING

King! You were created first just to rule the earth, not to be shackled, held down, or to be poisoned by anyone. Never to lay pilgrim to the polluted, tainted thoughts of others. As the king of the jungle you have the mighty roar of pride and protectant. Always enforcing your role as the king. Beating your chest, loving and protecting those that love you. A protector, ruler, lover, and bearer of life. Please select the right queen to be your wife. Full of pride, your eyes never lied, when it comes down to loving the queen. Yes, oh, yes, a true king indeed. Your strong hands pruned the nation, showing us the right direction. But, what about you? My king. Are you to live that way all of the time? Always fucking around with those unstable felines. Cheating, lying, grabbing, and killing. Is this what that pollution brings, to you as my king? Doom, gunfire, gloom, murdering your brother, crying, smacking your queens down, loneliness, leaving your tribe of prince & princess behind, just so you can make that fake gold coin dream in your mind. What is happening to you, my king? Your crown has now turned upside down. You have smelled that pollution and it has control. Greed has impeded that beaded brow to which I, your queen, was so proud. Your ruling your kingdom has slowly started to diminish. The proud lionly roar is now gone. You no longer can see what you are doing. Selling out your brother. Beating on your lover. Lying, cheating, stealing,

and killing. Is this what you want to be? Is this what a king should look like and be to me? I am not trying to put you down but only trying to make you aware what is truly going on out there in the eyes of your queens, prince, and princess. Please, O' please, don't die. For we can only survive in your domain.

WHY CRY

If life is sweet and love was new, life should have been right for you.

So why cry, God loves you, why cry! He'll do anything for you.

A baby so warm anew, I ask myself, was it for you so soft and sweet to smell, why, God? It feels like hell; I don't know what to say, but I pray for a better day, I should rejoice and sing praise for a new life, but also remember that lonesome night.

So, why cry when you're in good hands?

Why cry when you know God says he can?

FROM ONE TO ANOTHER

I enjoyed hearing from you, knowing you, wanting you, holding you, and maybe thinking about loving you.

You were a breath of new air for me. Making me live again. Stopping me from closing out the world from within!

> OH, What a Difference a Day Makes

You made me feel new again; somehow you took away my blues—WHEN I had no one else who cared for me. You dared to be the one for me. Somehow I felt our lives had just begun. You see?

> OH, What a Difference a Day Makes

Covering your hurt that I knew was there all along. Praying and hoping that you'll hold on and stay strong. I felt your need, surely I wanted to PLEASE!

> OH, What a Difference a Day Makes

But why, oh, why did this happen to me? To love another and desire me is a crime, so what kind of frame of mind were you in when you befriend thee?

> OH, What a Difference a Day Makes

From one to another brother you were wrong and it is now time for me to move on. Yeah, I know how you felt and what could have been. But why when I said I wanted you alone, my friend, you belonged to someone else? This pain cuts like a knife, because I don't want you out of my life.

As Billie says,

"Oh, What a Difference a Day Makes"

REMINISCENT OF YOU

As the creek rises and the curtains fall, as the sun shadows fall over trees. I think of you and me. No one can define our love. Somehow it fell apart in time; you still love me, I know you do, I do too. Can you feel it? I see it in you. With every ocean's curl, the way the sun rises and sets, you could almost bet what happened next. Like a soft whisper through the trees, I can still feel you calling out to me, I LOVE YOU! I think of you and sometimes cry, my heart drops, withers, and warps, and I feel I am going to die. Where, O, where, my love, can you be? I am calling out to you on bending knee. Hold me! Love me, like you used to do, without you I seem to cry and pray for you. I look at all of the things we have bought into our lives, and it breaks my heart and leaves a cruel path inside. As I take this journey I see I can't lie with all of the former loves from my past, I see no reason why. I can't...I can't love no one new, because all I am left with is a **REMINISCENT OF YOU**....

DOUBT

Father, my heart feels heavy. The place where I am is abusive but I have nurtured this thing and we have grown together. And here I am day after day with my eyes swollen and full of tears. My deepest fear is to let go.

STEP OUT ON FAITH... **Matthew 14:22-27**

I have prayed to you night after night about this. People tell me to have faith and pray everything will be okay.

HAVE FAITH! ... **MATTHEW 14:28-31**

I believe in you, Father. Yes, I feel you there and I know you have given me the peace I need to stand strong, but tell me something, is what I am thinking wrong?

STEP OUT ON FAITH...**MATTHEW 17:14-20**

Father, I can't take it anymore, please help me? Stop my tears and my fears from taking over me?

STEP OUT ON FAITH AND BELIEVE IN ME...**MARK 4:35-40**

My days are numbered now. I have set the date of my expiration to the place I have nurtured and grown with. I am ready to fly. I have accepted you and Lord, I do have faith. But I am afraid.

STEP OUT ON FAITH, MY CHILD... **MARK 6:5-6**

Oh, Father, thank you, thank you! I have a new place to grow and be nurtured. I have faith and with my faith in you the people around me felt it too. Without you, Lord, I would have drowned in my tears and fears. Without you, Lord, I would have no tomorrow. My heart is light with no more sorrow. How could I doubt you when you held me on my worst days? How could I doubt you when you wiped my tears and took the swelling away from my eyes and heart?

FAITH...**MARK 11:23**

Father, I will never doubt you again. For when things around me seem dark with a little candle lit, I won't cave in because I know that you are there and that you will guide me in.   **AMEN.**

ALONE

I entered a room full of people, laughter fills the air. I hear the clicking and chattering from the masses, those same people looking smug wearing one-eyed glasses. Though the room is full, I can't help but feel alone.... They greet me and smile. I grin but feel like a child in a big world full of adults covered with a lack of compromise and full of insults. They still have yet to capture my attention. But if sex were mentioned, that's a different issue altogether. So, I shall not fall victim to their prey, and all I can think is man, just go away. No, I'm not turning away, I am just looking for a place to stay and become stable in my day. The closer they get, the more I want to run. Just escape into a world of my own. Safe from harm, that's where I am ALONE.

ICE

One part water, make it twice as cold. Please, baby, place it on my body and make me lose control. Slowly, slowly rub it along my thighs and see me become hypnotized. Take it across my breast 'til you feel it's best that we not miss a spot. One could look at it as a diamond, so don't let it drop. For that one drop, that is known, as drip that leaves my tit will make me cry. To remedy that give it a suck, won't you try? OoooH! That feels so good on my clit, you make me want to cum, cum, cum slowly onto your lips. As my body starts to quiver from the cold, I look down at you and I know that time has not made you grow too old to stick it where it can hurt and please me, put it in, don't just tease me.

MY KING

MIGHT THEE EYES NEVER SWELL, MY LOVE. FROM THE MISTAKES MADE BY THEE QUEEN. SOMETIMES WITHOUT THEE, WHEN THEE LIFE IS DISMAL AND BLUE, THEE LOSE CONTROL AND SEEMS TO FELL WITHOUT YOU, 'TIS TRUE. NO, NOT IN GRADES NOR IN LIFE, BUT IN THE TRUE KNOWLEDGE AND REALIZATION OF YOU, THEE KING. THE TRUE KNOWLEDGE OF THE LOVE AND HEALING POWER THAT EXISTS, SOMETIMES GETS LOST DUE TO A SUBTLE TWIST OF FATE, BUT ALWAYS TRYING NOT TO LET THEE LOVE GET AWAY. I BEING THE QUEEN FEEL LONELY WITHOUT THEE KING AND SEEK NO REFUGE EXCEPT FOR THE POLICY OF BEING RUDE. FOR THAT WALL SHE PUTS UP IS FAKE AND TRYING TO HIDE IT FROM THEE KING, THERE IS NO ESCAPE. FOR HE SEES ALL IN THY EYES. THE EYES THAT CAN NEVER LIE TO THE TRUE LOVE OF HER LIFE. AS SHE NOW BEGS HIM, MIGHT I STILL BE YOUR WIFE! FORGIVENESS IS THE KEY. BUT ONLY IF THE KING DECIDES TO PARDON THEE. THAT RAIN SHALL NEVER COME ANYMORE, BECAUSE WHAT SHE HAS FOUND IN HER KING IS NO BORE. SO, AS THEE READ ON REMEMBER THEE SONG AND THAT HE AS MY KING IN MY HEART HE WILL ALWAYS BELONG. #1

SOMETIMES

You told me you
Sometimes you would hold me
Then shrug me off
If your love was so true,
then how come I am only 5% of you?
When you love someone you make them your world. That's what I do
      for you and I am still your girl. Too bad things cannot be equal.
      But please remember this, there will be no sequel.
My heart is broken and that's no lie, if only you can see how many tears
      I've cried. Man, o, man, I would be rich by now, instead I walk
      around carrying a frown.
Sometimes I wonder, was I stupid or just plain dumb, falling in love with
      someone who cannot show me their love, cannot show me they
      care, or better yet, just be there?
Always thinking of self, never me or, simply put, our new family. My
      heart is broken and that's no lie, but the thing I am going to say
      is no longer will I let life pass me by. You see, there will be others
      who I can consider better lovers.
                      So peep this,
                      I am out!

The Other Night!

Truly, truly I think of you. Many nights have come and gone and still I think of you. But I… I am still alone, how about you? The nights are at its coldest and hardest. My queen-size bed that sleeps two is uneven, for the lack of your presence.

Slowly, slowly I see our relationship starting to deteriorate. I don't know what to tell you now, because it seems too late.

Unlike **the other night**!

My love, my partner, the one I adore, you have left my life so abruptly. Don't you want me no more? I called you last night, you hung up. I want to see you, but I am left with no such luck. In the beginning we would see it all—together you and I, birds of a feather, yeah! We flocked together until your turncoat friends happened to interfere and overstep the welcome, bringing on many tears. Them with all their lies, cheating, and scheming! Now you're gone, left me still longing, longing, longing to love only you. Heck, I cried a few nights, then I said ah, the heck with you! Never looking back, knowing one day you'll regret the fact of your harsh decision to leave me. Yeah, I know no other girl can give you the same intensity as me. One thing I'll never forget is all that luggage you carried and yet I tried to help you forget. But now I think about that, that's one of my biggest regrets. No, loving you wasn't easy, no, not by far. But look at me now, baby! I'm a rising star. One day I know I'll find true love but I will never love a

man who carries luggage like he'd wear a suit. Like you did **the other night**!

FALLING ANGEL

When an angel falls
They hit cloud after cloud of
Pain and Ignorance
Abuse
Neglect, Pressure
Misunderstanding
Sin
Lies - Greed - Lust
The next last cloud
DEPRESSION
Danger
For without prayer & light
You'll hit

EARTH

Cycle of Life

When the world feels so right
That's when our love took flight
We embarked upon a journey that was to be everlasting.
But suddenly she came along and changed your heart.
Tearing my world apart! Some people call that the
cycle of life—cycle of love.

What's the meaning to the cycle of life—the cycle of love?

Does it always turn into pain? Does love remain? It seems real hard to be your friend now that our love has come to an end.

Cycle of life—cycle of love.

I am holding on for dear life, praying one day that I would be your wife. I thought our love was sent from up above! Tell me, how can a love so right be so wrong? I never understood 'til I heard our love song.

Cycle of life—cycle of love.

Don't let this be the end.

Cycle of life—cycle of love.

Saying Goodbye

Was he good for me
I thought he'd be
So strong tall and true
That's one of my reasons why
I fell
In love with you
'til you broke my heart!

Winter

It happened one winter's day when love drifted my way.
Like a snowflake I knew it was different and new.
Because he dared to utter the words
I LOVE YOU....

He touched my hand as I got a quiver
My eyes closed and my heart flashed
As I wondered, could I?

Could I love someone so new
This warm winter's love—'tis
True as winter come the forest
Becomes anew

And now so has my love for you

Impressions

Impressions are like footprints in the sands of time.
Sometimes when the waves come crashing they are washed away
With a semi-trace of the imprint on your heart
At other times a strong wind can come along and blow your prints away

With those two poor thoughts of impression
It's no wonder why a heartbreak lasts so long

Oh, how one step in your life can cut like glass
and make you bleed profusely
Sometimes those impressions last whether or not it's welcome
When that love touches your heart

Tender Heart

All my life I've looked for you
I know you're there 'cause I feel you
In my heart through and through

Sometimes when I cry at night—
it's because I am lonely and I am thinking of you!

You see, tender hearts need love too

Never turn me away, put me down.
For without you my world's upside down.

All I want is your love

Something to which is God sent from above.

Some may call it

Tender Heart

Sometimes!

There are times when we do something, we end up hurting one another

The look in your eyes—I see you're hurt so bad.

But baby, baby, please understand, it don't matter

Sometimes we can't see what's in front of us
Because we want to be loved so badly (sometimes we hurt ourselves)

But don't look back
No regrets!
Now!
Just try to hold on to what we have now.....

Love for self

Telephone Love

Part I

The Unknown

How can you miss what you never had?
What
A kiss that was never there
A touch that's soft as a rose
A smell so intoxicating that it sends you to another planet

How can you miss what you never had?
Was he ever yours or someone from your dreams? The pounding from his heart is like a pulse that pumps love into your life. Never to know how you feel or that he is the one.

Emptiness!

How can you miss what you never had?
Holding you close to him every night
Protecting you from all fears, while taking the time to dry your tears
Hearing the voice that sets your soul on fire
The voice that leaves you with one desire
Him

How can you miss what you never had?

Part II

SPIRITS

It seems like when two people meet that love has a chance to flourish. Some people want to call that person your soulmate, but in essence, they are your kindling spirit.

Looking at those two words
They appear to be the same. Behold, they are not.
Your soulmate is in another realm, but your kindling spirit exists here and now.
If a soulmate is what I seek, then I can wait.
For my kindling spirit needs me now.
I'll wait for the one who will give me my heart's desire.
The unconditional love
The perfectness that God has shown us that exists through our kindling spirits

Part III
HELLO

                                                          Hello!

I never met you before

                        But to hear your voice is never a bore

Life with you could never be—

          Because I am from another town, ya see!

                                      Our convo is so nice

Deep in my heart—

            You are a part of my life

Pardon me for being so forward, but my heart doesn't know the meaning of the word

               <u>STOP!</u>

So knowing how you feel about long-distance affairs, I'll make my exit and pretend you were never there.

             <u>GOODBYE!</u>

<u>(dial tone)</u>

VISION

As I close my eyes for the night
I know you
I feel you
We're like two comets starting to take flight.
I can feel your breath on my neck
I can hear your heartbeat like a conga drum as I lay upon your chest
I know you
I've known of you from day one.
I'll never forget that vision from which you come.
You have captured me and stolen my mind, body, and soul
Take me
You feel so real to be a vision
No one else can have me, but you
Know me
Take total control of our passions for each other
'till my dying day you'll be a part of me
my one true love you will always be
for I know you
I belong with you
No matter where you are or how far you may be
Your vision will forever cascade inside of me
For life
Vision (softly whispered)

Play Me

To play you is like something I've never experienced
As I place you in my mouth, I see I need to add a little moisture and heat to make you sound just right.
Listen
Listen
Listen to the sounds that you make as I blow and feel the heated vibrations on my lips.
The feel can be intoxicating.
The sound as I blow coming from your belly makes me feel alive with a sexual pleasure.
You're so deep!
No one can understand our togetherness.
Yes, I control the key to play you
But in the end it appears that you are truly playing me.

THE CRUSH

Every time YOU go by
Your scent lingers in the air
Your pussycat eyes sparkle and dance
Whenever you take the chance to
just smile

Your smile is all aglow
when I see you

I hope you know

DO YOU KNOW?

Can you tell that there is something in the air?

CATCH ME!

I'm falling from your dreadful stare.
Falling for you
Now, tell me
what's a girl to do?

Get to know me
I have a flava
A flava for you that is called
The crusH
(That's what I have on you)

YOU make me blush!
I almost have to catch my breath—when you arrive

I can't help but think about
The cruSH
The crUSH I have on
YOU have captured my curiosity
when you speak
All I can imagine is your lips calling out to me
Uttering—*kiss me!*
Your assurance has touched my soul
I meditate and yearn for us to connect
our two wandering souls
You better bet my heart is what you'll capture next
To measure it all—
The feelings
I have
Has their own terminal destination
It's simply called
The cRUSH!
To my generous estimation

Help me, please, with this CRUSH
I beg you.
Please!
Spare me no sympathy, please.
'Cause you see!
I have broken down on my knees after dealing and living in pain and agony
So, if you're not the one for me, send me a sign
And let me be
For I have no control of this thing

<u>*called*</u>

THE CRUSH

Ghost

I thought that I had let you go
But you keep hovering around me like some lost soul
It's been ten years and my heart has set a path trying to run from your thought and yet a last
Nothing
Ten years, it's been ten years
Ten years of tears that has set a fault
Please tell me why, every time I open my eyes in a glimmer I see you

I see you and I cry 10 x 2
You are like a ghost of Christmas past and hard to forget
I love you and I cry, it's not the same, when it's all done I hang my head in shame, for I am still in love with you
Never to find someone to replace you so I keep walking on on on

Walking until my feet have hard scars and corns
I steady myself and humble too, trying to find someone new, and every time I open my eyes there is you

As the winds blow and my shingles shutter I hold on to you, and I should know better
For one they aren't you trusting (not) and true

RIVER FLOW

People ask me why I cry
When my hands kiss the sky
I'm reaching out to hold you (Lord)
Holy love that comes aboard my soul
Makes my waters flow
Don't you know that he saved you
He gave you
Blessings and life
That river that flows from one is
My lifeline testimony
It's always warm—soothing
Thank you
Thank you
My river flows
No, it's not a path or road
It's where God is and wants
It to go
Thank you
Thank you
For my
River Flow

THE SWAN SONG

She is delicate
Her beauty unrefined
She is gentle in her movements
Never showing her flaws
Some people try to mimic her motions by wearing a designer label or fragrance (with no cause)
But no one can know her love
Who's to say that adorable swan doesn't have a song of her own.
For some would
Never know the sounds she makes could be a subtle moan
One would never guess unless they look into her eyes that look like coals.
That true image that allows you to see her soul
Sometimes her pain in her heart can burn like ferry.
But you will never know unless you hear her swan song.

LET'S TALK ABOUT LOVE

Let's talk about that four-letter word
That has a lot of different meanings
And what it means to me
I thought you loved me
People used that word out of content
but let's ask our Dear Lord for exactly what it was meant
I gave you the world and you seemed to trash it
But I loved you and where did it all go
And where all of my time with it

I Am Beauty

You!
Look at me. What do you see?
In your eyes do I appear to be some type of freak?
Do you not see my eyes that are as deep as the ocean's blue
My smile that can shine light and possibly control you
Come—hold my hands
Aren't they soft and warm
So some parts of me might not seem to be....
What's wrong?
Do you see something about me that makes you chuckle in sheer ecstasy
So what if my eyes aren't blue
So what if I appear big to you
Are you me? Obviously you cannot be, because I stand before you with dignity, pride, and grace. Grace upon the place I will never let you tread because if I do, you'll stick like glue and honey, I don't even want to go there with you.

Let me say first and foremost I
I am Beauty
I don't need fake hair, perms, and crystal rings,
for I am a real diamond if you can see.
I don't need to date hustlers who can't see beyond money. One who chases cash and ass and call his women bitches and not queens.
See me! Now taste me, I am bittersweet. I make all bees come after me. I don't need plastic surgery like the "Queen Bee." See, I am me and me being me makes me
BEAUTY!

Who Are You

I just met you and already I feel a bond
I will never be able to explain it
because all I know is due to my excitement
you might be gone

Who Are You
Why?
Why must you grace my presence with your catalytic ways?
I can't understand why I feel petrified with the joy of knowing you.
You have cornered my soul my defenses are down and I am left trotting
And sauntering (dance) around with a mere image of you

Who Are You
Why have you come?
I know I am not in love and at times I want to run
But this feeling I have for you
I hold near with kid gloves

You have pierced my heart where the pain used to be with utter madness of you
That is truly unexplainable

Who Are You
Are you my gallant knight in shining armor?
Are you the unknown soldier who's come
To help me over the pain and doubts
Please, all I need is for you to help me out

WHO ARE YOU

FREEDOM

Look at me, do you like what you see?
I was born just for him, for it is he who
created me.
He blessed me and made me a sight to see. Can you catch me?
Through life you'll see me as one thing, to which in some people's eyes
does not seem appealing
But as time goes by I grow up into a beautiful creature for all to see

Look at me, do you like what you see?
Please, stop trying to capture me.
For if you do, what is it that you expect of me?
To control my small body locked in a decorative frame
suffering from excruciating pain.

Let me go, I just want to be free
To fly from your garden and perhaps to be in a fruit tree.
For my life is short lived and I have only begun
So keep your repugnant hands off of me or I will be done
Done too soon
Because I only have searched for my freedom

TRUTH

Here I am again
Alone in agony
Sitting around pondering about what could it be

We had a lot in common except
for the liking of me.

I figured we had problems once he stopped calling me

How come a person can't call you and tell you the truth?

The truth is the most, easiest thing
the truth won't have you relying on that string that's connected
to that thing you call a telephone

if only they knew that the truth hurts less than a lie
which could never justify my
tears I hold inside

I have one thing to ask you, my friend

When the time comes, will you lie to me again?

TRUTH!

GONE

What was once lost is your love for me
You could not see the flower that blooms and exists within me
At one time I refused to smile
Until
I realized you were acting like a child
You tried to run me down with your petty jealousy,
but failed to see the strength that was
growing inside of me

So you stomped out of my life like a shoe to a bug
And now you want to come back

Check behind you, forward and back
As you look around and see that the sunshine I gave you is no more
It feels colder now because I love you no more

Open those big brown eyes of yours and see
You can walk over me no nevermore
For I am gone just like yesterday and the day before

Gone! Gone! Gone! And never no more!

friend

They smile in your face
Talk behind your back
The unsurpassable amount of disrespect is
strong enough to give you a heart attack
As a matter of fact, looking back
I can never describe you as a true-blue friend
'Cause every time I see you
you have the chaser's cat grin

always chasing after what I have

Dream Thief

I have dreams of a life that the Lord has given to me
Yet you come and break into my house when my mind is free and
you try to steal from me
Leaving me confused
Used and torn about
Who I am
Where will I be
And is this from the God above
For this is not done out of love
This is the dream thief who wants to kill, steal, and destroy
You have come to turn my family against me
Come to stop me from loving those who love me
But God
Yes, but God has given me the power to case you out in Jesus
now
Now feel my power that my Father has given me
Know he loves and if I am quiet and still I will always hear him
Yes, you dream thief, I may be down but I am not out
You come and creep like a thief in the night

Quest or Question

If someone asked me
To explain my love for you
I would say…

Picture a plane crash in the desert. No food, no water, and no shelter.

According to my compass my love wouldn't be too far away.
So, I'll run to him—for whatever comes my way.

Without him I'll die….
It's like trying to quench that thirst
from the illusion that the desert provides

if I drink of him just this one last time
my lifeline would be replenished forever in a lifetime

A WALK

I took my first step and you were there
I ran from you and you cried
I peed in your bed out of fear
You laughed and loved me

I took another step—my second step
As it would be
As I grew I never understood your
Pushing, working, and prepping me
For this game called life

I took another step—my third
You looked at me and shocked me
When you said I love you
I rolled my eyes because
You taught me when I didn't want
To learn

I took another step but this time
I stumbled
And you told me that's okay
I'm proud of you anyway

My next step was big in its own
Way—hey, it's graduation day
Oh, you bragged because you were proud—so
I say to you, Grandma, look at me now
I can walk!

I AM...

Tell me, what would you do if
People mistreated you?

took advantage of you
poisoned you
trashed you
suffocated you
simply killed you

What would you do
Keep taking care of them
Love them
Provide shelter
Nurture them

I don't know—I DON'T KNOW
I have kicked you out of tides
Rained on your life with my tears
Crumbled around your feet
Exhaled as hard as I can
And I still don't have your attention

Just who in the hell are you to do this type of cruelty to me?

When I have been your providing life
Giving you light
Clean water and air

Who am I, you ask?
Who am I, you ask?

I AM EARTH

I was made for you
You are a part of me
You came from me
As you have blood so do I
As you cry so do I
As you breathe so do I

Take down your crap
That surrounds my being
Stop trashing me as you walk
Stop poisoning me with your chemicals

STOP
STOP
STOP
FOR I AM

YOU

I DREW A BLANK

I drew a blank
What can I say
I shop every day
For new words to say

Dag it!
Help my mind get clear
When I drew a blank—'cause
There are words I want to hear

New words
Old words
Big ones
little ones too

I must keep writing so I'll have something to do

I drew a blank!

150 words
I must say for you to hear and maybe cheer me!
But I drew a blank today

HIP!!!!   HIP!!   HOORAY!!!!

MEOW

MEOW
MEOW

I am on the prowl
Can you love me now

Meow
Meow

I'll jump up and
I'll jump down
Just to see if you can love meow

I'll purr for you
I'll rub on you
Meow, now tell me what can
you do now

Ah AAhhh AA ACHEWWWW!

Is that what you have for me
I just had your hard hairy legs on me
I said I was here for you
And that's what you have
to offer

MMMMEEEEOOOOWWWW!!!!

The Ways

Let me count the ways to love you

One, if I hold your hands does that make you want me
When I kiss your lips did you know you make me wet
Let me learn how to love you;
I want to bite you on your lips
Wiggle my hips on top of your tip;
caress your manhood with my tongue
Baby, slow don't run—
I will bite
Just let me learn how to love you tonight
Do you like my scent
Does it turn you on with this short time we have spent
I never want to do you wrong.
Let me love you right
How 'bout making it tonight
Do you mind if I took a nibble here and a nibble there
And a touch—look at you
So beautiful with every glance
Have I counted all of the ways for our romance?

Let me count the ways to love you

Do you want me to stop
I didn't think so, let me reach the top
The top of your love with every stroke

ODE TO TOUCH

A soft, gentle breeze
A cottony feel
Soft velvet caress my skin
The warmth of a graze upon my hand
is all I think of when a tear falls
To be held so close, I can heart your heartbeat

A kiss upon my neck would be twice as sweet

Hold me
hold me with tears I cry

Ode to a touch
I dream of by and by
Can I not be held, I fear I'll die
Without touch
without love
One day I'll be fine

ODE TO TOUCH

BLESS IT!

I want this night to be the night
Over centuries you have forgotten
For a lifetime I've been waiting
I know you like the sky
From the heat of the day
'til the cool of the night
Remember me and what I am to you
Feel my heat, feel my pleasure
Accept my love as an endless treasure
Don't doubt what you've been given
Only the heavens above is worth this, your intention
Open your heart and stretch out your arms
The love I give has boundless charms
All I ask is for you to know me
Love me and
Accept me

GET OUT OF MY WAY

As I speak to you today
I say get out of my way

Over the years you have tried to hold me down
You have made me cry
Until I nearly wanted to die
You have stolen from me
You have tried to block me and my dreams

I thought it may be a plot or even a scheme
Until I realize that I was who can stop me

I've gotten on bended knees and said,
"Mountain, get out of my way.
I'm thanking my Lord today."

I Dream a Cloud

Upon a bed of clouds I lay
Pondering about my day
Was it good or was it bad
I dream of what I had
On my plate with my date
Step by step these clouds survive

My confusion—my delay
of which direction
I'll make today

Shall I run or shall I drift
My decision must come quick

Some clouds have holes in them
But yet it's just a dream
I'll reply
with the lack of no decision
I rely—just adrift
but never still this wonderful life is filled—

I dream a cloud

Your Dance

Jump up
Get down
Now shake your booty around

If your love is steady
Shake your confetti
And groove

Groove to the beat of love
It rocks you off of your feet

So jump up
Get down

Show the world your style
Don't hold back, just looking at
your heart beating steady
you know that this time
you're ready
for a real love affair

STORM

Roving around high in the sky
You rumble, crumble with flashes of light
Tears of rain take flight

A CHILD AT PLAY

Cold air all around me
The white flakes gripping astound me
Like a child I play

CAPTIVATING

Look there, my full moon
Shining so bright, making me swoon and yet
Touching my heart so right

Who Dream

I keep seeing you every night
I know I feel you holding me tight
It's never just for one night
It feels like every day of my life
You kiss me—with lips so soft
You touch me—with hands so strong
You say you love me and I know it's true
I too am in love with you
But at last I open my eyes and you aren't there
to my surprise
A dream I wish was real
a halo over your head
I must deal—for you are in my
dreams every night and that is where
our love takes flight
But in my heart and in my mind
I long to know who are you
my love divine.

DO YOU REMEMBER

There was a time when
we used to laugh together
have fun with one another

Have you forgotten?

The sky was the limit and you, my
friend, and I were in it to win it

No one to stop us—no one to kill our joy

We cheered and shouted, oh, boy,

Have you forgotten?

Now my chips are down;
I cry and often wear a frown
I try to cheer like a clown
But can you see that the clown's smile is now upside down?

Have you forgotten me?

My pains sound loud
I dream of ecstasy
No, not a place but a state of mind
Where no pain can continue to bind nor intertwine my body and mind

Do you remember me?

I was your friend, the one

at times we tried to see if we could really be blood relatives

Do you remember me?

That's okay, for now I am here to say I am free of worry and grief
I really don't need your cheer; all I wanted was you to be here
So, if you don't remember me
Try looking in the mirror, then you'll see
I am gone and now you're all alone, where you wanted to be

Because now I am happy and I am free

THE FORGOTTEN PEOPLE

Some are old
Some are badly injured
Some have life but want to end it

They never ask for much, all they want is your time
But when you need something
They come first to your mind
Why do they cry when no one is around?
They appear happy but their hearts wear a frown upside down

Do you really care?

They are human just like you
They comb their hair and brush their teeth just like you
But you are nowhere to be found

We live in a world of forgotten people
They are just like you and me
But we treat them as ghosts easily

We see no expression, not even a glance
it would be easy if they had a chance
to shine in our eyes like glory divine
as we do in their eyes all of the time

Some are old
some are crippled
some are young
some are angry
and some are through
if you look around some are just like you

PINKY DINKY DINK

Pinky dinky dink, you stink
Pour me into the river
and see what color
ink I'll be

my heart runs a river of
red
pink
gray
and
blue

let me show you how much
I love and think of
you

Pinky inky dinky ink
you stink

My Christmas Love

*If counting the day of Christmas could show
you my love
there would never be enough days
in a year.*
Merry Christmas

LIVE IT

Everyone is doing it
and yet we go through live without acknowledging it
It exists, but yet we go about so free
in a sense we think, *It won't happen to me*
Life is so delicate
yet we harbor anger, anguish, stress, and hate.
Why?
When we can sit back, love, and relax while the time goes by
LIVE
Just like the hands on a clock, there isn't much time to be ignorant
It's time to grab hold
Get out of your bed and let it be said
You did it
You achieved it
And now you know what to do with it
SHOUT!

My Friend

There you sit looking brand new
I never knew how true you held us too, our friendship was like the ocean blue
On good days we would sail right through, the clouds were clear and the sky was blue

My Friend

I didn't know I had a great friend like you
When the storms come and you know they do—the oceans seemed rough and tossed you and your crew. My anger roared at you and like a sea captain you saw us through

Yeah, you would pick on me and you know you do. You keep me strong so now I hang on to you. Don't leave me when my storms are strong, because my best friend you will always be.

Please, O please, my friend
Please remain in my life as my family and friend

I'll hang in there with you. I know no one can, they say you were untrue and this is how I see you.

My friend

RSD
(Reflex Sympathetic Dystrophy)

I walk through the world in a wounded haze
while my life is a maze of drugs and tears

I feel alone, helpless, lifeless, and confused
No friends can hold me, no one can touch me
No one who understands this pain from within

My heart says be free, run, and be me.
The pain consumes me, the drugs they lose me.
My mind is gone, along with some memories of yesterday.

Yesterday has come and gone, now some memories say so long.
My heart weeps for someone to love.
My body yearns to be held but I am alone.
Walking in this cloudy haze.
Longing for a way to be me—to be free of

RSD

At times I'm angry, sometimes I am sad.
But I ask myself, why not try something else instead?
Know you have God,
know you live,
know you have family

RSD

I'm going to fight!

PARTY OVER HERE

I am here
    start up the band
        'cause here I am

Some thought that they could
stop me and hold me
back

But I got the power of love and you can best believe that

He pulled me through all of your hateful lies
while wiping the tears from my soulful eyes

It's time to celebrate
because I am here to stay
God's love
has helped me find my way
no depression today

It's time to celebrate!

HOW DO YOU

I know I shouldn't feel this way
I mean, you are the one I hold dear and
help me see things clear
you always hold me when I'm uptight
just to make it through the night

How do you know that the sky is blue?
How do you say to a friend?
I love you

I've always called you when I was feeling blue
just like an angel you pulled me too

How do you know that the sky is blue?
How do you say to a friend?
I need you

Just like that diamond in the sky
You've captured my heart—my soul
I have no idea why I haven't told

How do you know that they are birds that fly?
How do you say to a friend?
I am here for you, so don't cry

Shall I hold out my hands to you?
Will that be enough for you?

HOW DO YOU

I'M A WARRIOR

You beat me and pound me
you work all night. You just wanna make me
cry so I won't take flight

But that's all going to end
 right here and right now

Because I'm a warrior

Well, you beating and pounding
I'm praying all night
'cause I'm a warrior

You think all of your cheating
Will break me, that's not right

Because I'm a warrior
I put God first before I take flight

I'm a warrior
You'll get knocked down
Starting tonight

Because I'm a warrior

No time for repeating, you know the reason
That I'm a warrior
Yes, I got the power
Why
'Cause I'm a warrior
It's my season

LETTERS OF LOVE

A = Amor
B = Beautiful
C = Creation
D = Dedicated
E = Elegant
F = Fantasy
G = Grace
H = Heavenly
I = Intriguing / Intimate
J = Joyful
K = Kind
L = Love
M = Meaningful
N = New
O = Open
P = Pleasure / Passion
Q = Quality
R = Romance / Ravishing
S = Satisfying / Scrumptious
T = Trust
U = Unveiled
V = Valuable
W = Wise / Worm / Wanted
X = Xanadu
Y = Yenning
Z = Zing

LOST

Lord, I see ya walking with me
Lord, I see ya even talking to me
Lord, at times I tell ya I'm lost
And it's hard at times when I forget you're the boss

I'm Lost

So what do I do
My mom says read Psalms 91

But I hear you're saying relax and let go

Then you say I'll be running your show

now it seems my bad luck has changed
and
now I go around shouting your name

hallelujah!   hallelujah!

Amen

WHO AM I

Who am I
I am the woman that struts her stuff
and everywhere I walk
I find a new fan

Who am I

With a twinkle of an eye and a slight graze
of my thigh
honey, your man is mine

I can lick my lips, switch my hips, and you know what?
I got him…
I got your man

Who am I

Ask him about my scent that was on him last night

Who am I

I am every breath he'll take and the love he'll make—with me

I have stolen your man in the night, as well as the daylight.
Sometimes I think I might give him back…
NOT!

Who am I

I am you

Deep down and true blue....

No, I am not a whore but I just want what's yours and possibly a little more,
how 'bout it?

Tonight

Why is the sky so beautiful tonight
Is it because He embraces my heart's deepest delights

The way the moon leads a path along the sea, I can't help but think He has made that path just for me

With the soft touch of His shine
He informs me that His true love is divine

Though I reach out to grab the moon, I can't touch it. But I can feel it! That shine is so strong

I do know that it is His love gracing me in the night. It glistens with such radiance that it touches my soul. With love so bold it will never grow old

No one seems to know the pleasures He brings
 but if you look Him up
you will see His shining ring of love

US TWO

We are two circles that collided
Those were dreams like suicide
We continue to go 'round and 'round
Like a top hat turned upside down
We spin and spin like a top on an electric cloak you push
Stop!!!
So we won't choke

But once we hit there is no turning back
Though we must watch out for the black cat

Once we give have hit and spun
A bottomless pit of desire
Fire! Fire!
We go deep like a kaleidoscope, we see the
Difference we spun

Version of our love no one can change from
above
but as in history shall it remain

My Seed of life

You plant a seed to watch it grow
All along not knowing which direction it may go

You water and talk to it night and day
'til you start to notice it's starting to stray

Why you cry and scream as soft as a butterfly flies

Nowhere to hide the heavy tears as they flow

I hear a knocking, my, who could it be

Now you have disrupted my flow, now you have to go

Though it's hard to say goodbye
To something you've yearned for, so try not to lie.

Dry those tears that's caused you such pain
unlock that side of you that's going insane.
Realize the love in you.
Know there is someone in heaven protecting you

They planted you and watch you grow
Never giving up on you
And now you know what to do, continue to your quest knowing all along you've done your best in life and after

Smile because the sun is shining, smile because your seed is astounding
It will grow as you wished, but knowing you haven't given up on it will be the prize before your very eyes.

Watch Your Mouth

Look at those lips, so beautiful and true, it's hard to believe what comes out of you.
You were once a delight in your momma's eye
Now all day she sometimes sits around and cries, wondering where your mouth has gone. When will it return home? You were the seed that spoke with complete joyful beauty and such flair, with a smile that fell upon your face in every space. Never knowing what disgrace you would spew out of your vessel of life. You are my seed, how can this be a part of me?

With your shouting out explicit vulgar words and telling numerous lies which could always be heard with all of the cursing and a whole lot of thrusting (your body) for what you claim is respect and not boosting for all of the world to see—and some as yet

It's hard to believe you come from inside of me

You better watch your mouth—do you hear me? It's hard to change what's been spoken out loud and with your tawdry vocation pointing from every location of the body you claim you are my child.

You speak out with no expectations of a rebuttal and always want to fight when you have created a huddle of onlookers, hookers, and more, never realizing after last night they considered you their whore. Yet your mouth speaks so proudly with defaming glow. As your mother watches her knees started to buckle below. She shakes her head and wonders how, still no answer, you can't be my child.

As your disrespect creeps out even more, all of the people around you know 2 + 2 equals 4 makes you appear to be even more intolerable, lacking of sophistication and nothing to adore. Your mother pleads with you, never no more speak in such disgrace, and yet you disrespect her right to her face.

I can say no more but watch your mouth.

It can get you in a world of trouble and possibly get you locked down with whom you've called the devil. In that place where there is no space for that gentle touch you loved so much and no more lullabies when you say goodnight to your fellow inmate.

You better watch your mouth

As time goes by your mother often wondered why, with tears gentle falling from her sad swollen eyes. Someone replies to her saying: no, the reason for every season a fruit will fall. Causing all of that damaging language could only fall from that family tree, which is a part of thee. So watch your mouth as your sprouts begin to grow

Don't let that ugly sight flow. Think before you speak and you may preach a word of wisdom that lies underneath of that devil's peak on your tongue. Please watch your mouth you will find it's not fun. WATCH YOUR MOUTH

REPUTATION

Reputation
Reputation
A celebration of
Reputation

Reputation leaves devastation of/from a situation that had no need of existing
We are all in search of the right one but because we know nothing, so we repeat it time after time.

Reputation
Reputation
Reputation
Borders on frustration

Always in search of but never finding, our brains become intertwining due to lack of simplicity. We all feel the need to be repetitious and never unwinding. Our brain cells keep on twining due to us never being free to be expressive. And in time it manifests itself the right entity only showing to be …

Reputation
Reputation
Reputation

FORGET IT!

YOU SAID IT ALL

Last night, you said it all
Last night
Your words were loud and strong
Without thinking your words
Went thinking
Ringing with that
Power
They were hot and loud
Stunned the crowd
Last night
You said it all last night
Last night
I couldn't put up a fight that night
As you went burn
Barreling hot into my chest I closed my eyes
Praying for rest
Last night…
You said it all last night
I feel my breath
I feel the breath of my
Heartbeat, longing to hold on
So slow, so slow
So disconnected sometimes
Like a beat of a song
Last night, you said it all
Last night
You wouldn't put up a fight
With my love light leaving

My shadow light gleaming
My life echoes in a balance with one more
Beat
Because you said it
All last night

For So Long

For so long I have healed you
For so long I have known you
No one could ever tell me you'll do me wrong

My eyes have never seen so much love

My heart felt a kiss from above

So gentle, so warm
For 9 years my heart was torn
Because
for so long my heart was sworn
To love

Which leaves me now to say

So long, lost love

It was warm, young love, and now
I am…
I have grown
My love and now I have learned more from love

So now and forever you are my love
For so long

I will never forget love
And all that hasn't come of yet

FOR SO LONG

WHAT

What was that
The soft, moistened touch upon my face

What was that
A pinch of knowledge that won't go to waste

What was that
your guidance without a care

What was that
You fighting off every nightmare

What was that
When you let go of my hand and taught me to fly

Now why I cry, I need you once more

What was that
You held me and told me you'll love me anyway

So wipe away my tears, you say in your heart I will forever stay

There is no need to ask, what's that?
Anymore because you are grown now and you know

How much I

Love and adore…YOU…

WHAT!!!!! (smile)

Tell Me Something

How can a person say you don't
matter

Their words sounds like mere
chit-chatter

that can shatter the earth's ground
that rocks the
foundation
we call
family

Aren't you an Adam in all
degrees?
God picked first
to serve Mother Earth for me
and as a child you would hear

My pitter-patter and a cry
and would hold me to the sky
and say it will be okay

Because I am your Daddy
I am here to stay in your dreams

So please
Tell Me Something

Where would you be if it
weren't for ...

FATHER

Look at YOU
How can one be so rare?
So beautiful
you touch my life with such a sweet, tender smell
I look at you without a touch
because I can crush your soft, tender
petals
I feel I want to protect you from the harsh winds of life.
So I'll cover you with the
Kiss of love and life

A new day is ahead with stronger winds
Yes, you were put on this earth with thoughts of natural protection
'Tis your elegance and grace that calls for one's affections

From sunup to sundown I look at you and cannot help
but smile at the works that nature has abound

Look at YOU

Still standing throughout the heavy rainstorms
Still intact, one could learn a lesson from that
and you still stand with no thorns

Look at YOU

Love Affair

Love is like a crystal glass, some marvel at it,
some just think it's just glass
Look at its cuts and all of the curves it makes;
look at the light reflecting rays' dances
all around with uninterrupted joy
a dance that one would die to take and enjoy
like a grapevine love sometimes
All that makes a person long for you

Ummm!!!!
Taste wine, soft music
strawberries
chocolates
all that makes a person long for you

Your smile is bright like the moon's
reflection off of still waters
I want to stare you

Your eyes twinkle like diamonds
Diamonds that'll make a rich man
MAD
I want to hold them

As I get to know you I feel there is no way
to control the passion that burns
within
please quench it

From your strong, bulging chest to the firm
roundness of your ass, I wanna grab
and feel it when I pass
it's a love affair that you just can't grasp

Recognize me

Was I lost or some type of mystery
You'll see, open them eyes and smile
with me, enchanted and fantastic
Recognize me
Set me free
I've just been on a journey
for which you'll need to see
So recognize me
don't you see
if you'll look in the
mirror your heart will
fill with glee because
you'll see the one
who I recognize is
me!

Clouds

In my tower I sit so high
I see every cloud floating by.
As I gaze I feel lifted and
one
As we float by
why
can quench
the sun with our love and adoration
This cloud is a castration of nature's
balance with the sky

I enjoy floating by until I hit
the fluffy clouds and make it rain
feeling the rapture from it can be an
energy drain unless you see it
as an individual well…
who dare not
go insane
wasting time, causing pain
so grab a chair with me
and just sit and stare with me
as clouds float by

Journey

As I walk on my journey
I see my path
How long it is, the road is hard, filled
with coverages
Unnoticed nor requested this path
My talk is not the best, yet
I still walk on my journey
my heart led astray, never knowing
where
the sunset will lead at the end of the day
I walk fast
I walk slow
I walk hard and yet my heart just wants to continue to go
because I know that there is a golden pot at the end of the rainbow over-
flowing with
dreams, love, and more
than I could ever conceive
Boy, this journey has already set me free like that eagle that flies high
above the sea to the mountains....
Yeah, that could be me!!!!
So I will keep on my journey

I LOVE YOU

You're so cold and strong
You're hitting my tired arms
as blistering as you may be
I hear you calling for me
but I love you

Why hasn't time
quenched that desire that
makes your insides
melt

This empire that you sought for
us was no more
we get off our elevators on
different floors

but why and how is it
that when I open my doors
it's sheer kismet
you hit me and I'm down
for the count. I can't breathe, rescue me
you say I love you

HELLO!!!!

I never met you before
but to hear your voice is
never a bore.

Life with you could never be
because I am from another town
yeah see!

Our convo is so nice deep in my
heart—you're a part of my life.

Pardon me for being so forward
but my heart doesn't know the
meaning of the word
<u>STOP</u>

So knowing how you feel about long-distance
affairs I'll make exit and
pretend you were never there.

GOODBYE!!!!

SPECIAL

You make me enjoy the morning air when I'm with you—your eyes—you sparkle like diamonds when we walk side by side, there is a rhythm in our step that beats like a song that no one can hear but us.

When our hands touch there's a surge that strikes like lightning during a hurricane that makes people run for cover.

When we kiss it's like the moon dancing with the ocean—when there's no one to stop us
You touch my heart and make me feel as if we are one, that is why I sing this song, you make me feel so special.

Your embrace—uummmm, yummy. So strong, you turn me on all day, all night, I just can't sleep without you here tonight, all because you make me feel so special.

Oohh! Baby, grab me, don't let me go, touch me, just the thought of you makes me blush—all because you make me feel so special.

HOW ARE YOU

There I find myself constantly thinking of you.
Wanting to reach out and love you.
I digress!
For you are not real.
My passion for you is a demise to my life.
If I can't touch you
However, I can feel your thoughts, your tenderness,
I cry at the lack of adoration.
Is it my size that sways your love for me?
Is it my eyes that scare you?
Trust me, I am as beautiful outside as I am in.
Now don't think every time I talk to you
I'm flirting because on the real all I want to know
Is
HOW ARE YOU

ANGEL CRIES

When an angel cries it's felt in the heavens above. Their pain just rocks the earth. Their tears are like acid to the spin, it takes you out of your frame of mind. The pain so sharp it can cut the cord of a harp. With no one to understand, we tend to pay them no mind.

When an angel cries no one can hear their song because it's beautiful. NO one knows their pain or sorrow.
Why, oh, why they cry through their throbbing pain?

Tell me, please, why is this world so insane? People are so insensitive to (others') one's needs. My heart bleeds because of the crazy disease called "me first." That's when nothing else matters, life can be hard. Stop that darn chit-chatter.

When an angel cries her wings seem to sink into sadness. The darkness sound of loneliness creeps and sets upon them.

When Angels Cry…

When angels cry it seems to kill their souls. In their eyes songs from the heaven were told their joy and laughter filled our hearts, who knew it would bring on darker pastures? With no love, we would only feel pain. With no touch, we miss out on the softness.

DIFFERENCES

We were placed on this earth to be unique.
When he shaped us there was a simple heartbeat.
The heartbeat of the minds in unison sounds like chimes
We, meaning you and me
Our love seems like it will never be
I know you love me and me of you.
But with those subtle differences, what are we to do?
For you see, this is my plea from me to you.

No one can tell what our future will bring
but I just don't see that
Diamond ring.
You have touched my heart
love at first sight, nah, not by far.
We have a connection of the minds, heart, body, and soul
Please help me, before you go.
Show me how much you love me.

For we cannot bring a closure to our love without saying goodbye
in such a way that will make us cry.
The joining of those mere parts is the reason why.
We cannot let go without sealing it with a kiss, or whatever else it
may come with.

Thank you for asking me to be your wife
I will remember this for the rest of my life
Oh, how I wish this could be
I being your wife and you being with me

As for now all I feel is my heart fading and dying
when it used to be flying

Flying high up on the clouds as free as could be
I wonder what life would have been for you and me

TIME ZONE

What was of yesterday is no longer of today
Today will no longer be yesterday
Hence today and yesterday are the same

My friends, we are stuck in the timezone

YOU

Y – Youthful

Your beauty is forever young. Your smile will seduce the smallest creature. Your eyes sparkle like the brightest star. No wonder astronomers become confused with you constellations. Your looks are always anew. That is why I can see the youthfulness of you.

O - Onyx

Your heart is as pure as the onyx. If everyone knew your worth, no one could afford your grace. There would be wars over you that no one could ever win. You are as smooth as the onyx. Always full of illumination.

U – Unchangeable

No one can stop your perfection. No one can change the love you have to offer. No one can control the flower that you are. You have the strength of a whale and the gentleness of a butterfly. You are unchangeable, forever and always. There is one more thing I need say, please stay that way.

Stich

Our eyes locked
and I knew
you
would be mine forever
but who knew as we grew
we would be like a needle and thread
going in and out of each other's lives
like the fabric of time

COLOR

Man, cut shit out, all of those negative words coming out of your mouth about my color. What's it to you even if I were black and blue? If when you cut me I bleed red. If you look at me I have a head, with features just like yours—so what in the hell are you harling about color for? I have a mother and father just like you, and if you look any closer you might think I look just like you. Yes, some are light and dark but we all are from the same Bub—Adam was his name, stand up, be proud from whence we came. Because in the dark we all look the same. So what is color but a name?

GET OUT OF MY WAY

As I speak to you today
I say get out of my way
Over the years you have tried
to hold me down
you have made me cry
until I nearly wanted to die
you have stolen from me, you have tried to block me and my
dreams
I thought it may be a plot or even
a scheme
until I realized that I was who can stop me
son, I gotten on bended knee and say
MOUNTAIN
get out of my way
I am thanking the LORD today
for just being able to say
GET OUT OF MY WAY

LET'S CELEBRATE

I am here
start the band
'cause here I am

some thought they could
stomp on me and hold me
back

but I got the power of love
and you can best believe that.

He pulled me through all of your hateful
lies while wiping the tears
from my eyes.

It's time to celebrate
because I am here to stay.

God's love has helped me find my
way, no more depression today.

It's time to celebrate, let's do that today.

JUST THE WAY YOU ARE

People may talk behind your back
but I see in your eyes who you really are.
Nothing can change the beauty
that flourishes from inside those big beautiful eyes.
Just the way you are
I'll accept you just the way
you are.

Whenever we're apart
Just the look and the feel of the southern skies
reminds me of your warmth
your spirit is warm
along with your hugs
when I think of you it's like heaven's little gloves.

So you're not perfect or a supermodel
but if they knew you the world
would try to follow that glimmer of love in heart
that's why it's easy to
accept you that you are.

I've Lost My It

Damn, it's lost and nowhere
to be found.
Are you there?
Have you searched everywhere?
I've lost my it and it's nowhere
to be found....
I've walked for days
town to town
drowning in my own sorrows with my head hanging down.

Looking under rocks
climbing up every tree
screaming out every name and
I still can't seem
to find my it.
Will it be, will it be
that I shall never see my it?
Because, you see, I have lost my it
and but if I take a look back, hey!
It's still in me!!!

MOON

Moonlight
Moonlight, I pledge to thee a former love who watched over me
you have guided us through the night with the twinkling stars that
gleamed in with sheer delight
O, how I long for another moonlit night
but I must digress in my sorrowful tears that stream tonight
My moon, my moon, I loved them, so why is it when you glow I see a
single seat sitting in one row? O, gentle moon, will it be another for me?
That sparkled as bright as thou did thee.
Please guide me through one more love, please
I'm counting on you.

If not, I know one day you'll be twinkling with the stars
with a love for me on that day once more.
Maybe not today
but on another night that is as beautiful as tonight.

JUNKYARD

Now, since you are my best friend, can I play around in your backyard

We are close as close can be
so I know you believe and trust in me

But when turn your back I got you, Jack
I can dig up every bone
and call them my own

As we play in your backyard

Yes, you told me about the other talent wagers who tried to take your faves
but I too have played with your bones, you have strayed away.

You have called that your junkyard of bones
I'm sure you will hear me moan as I screw them behind your back
Because why?
I am your best friend.

 You gather with former lovers,
I will visit you too and dare to claim one or two while I play in your junkyard

I am your best friend, or so I say!

MY SISTERS

I woke up this morning and I heard a word that sat me back and made me cry. Why, O, why must I hear a sound that tears us down? When I know that we once walked, adorned with crowns like Nefertiti, Isabella, nor would Elizabeth have stood for the mess we say or do. Now tell me, how can you go around allowing yourself to fall from GRACE and Glory? When God put you in a place of being the first female to walk the earth, named Eve, and now you're allowing someone to call you beneath thee. Take a good look at your mother, she gave you life. So know now you can be someone's one wife.

So, you're not someone's BITCH!!!!! No, sir… no, sir, you're not a bad-ass bitch…. Whatcha call me? I'm the biggest, baddest BITCH! I said because everyone else says it, it's the in thing.

So, how do you see me? Am I your bitch? What you call me? Get a grip, a reality check. Because just like fashion, you're out of style, child. I'm no bitch, just because. I'm no bitch out of love. I'm a queen and don't drag me through your negativity, because I know who I'm meant to be and I say it righteously.

I'm a queen, I'm not your bitch.

Some of you are wearing the word "bitch" as a badge big, proud, screaming it and shouting it out loud. "I'm the baddest bitch you'll ever know."

But isn't that what some of our ancestors groaned about a four-legged pet? Yes, you bet! They called a dog that but yet you call yourself a bitch, and now I don't think a dog would even like that title themselves. Why, she was a female and was disrespected in the same, in just with that title you want to remain.

MY SISTERS, I'M NOT A BITCH

There used to be a time when we would fight when people called us by that name, and yet we are proud to be called the same.

I AM NOT A BITCH

MY SISTERS, I AM NOT A BITCH (please repeat this to yourselves)
What happened to being called the queens we are like Nefertiti, Sheba, Isabella, Amina, and your mother, y'all?
My sisters!

THAT'S JAZZ

Bah Boom Click, Click, Click...Bah boom click, click, click,
Goes the muddy rhythm of my heart with that satin tone, you make my nights swirl with your love.
I can't help but think of you, the strong melody of the vibrations upon my lips sends a stormy sensation down my legs and hips to stomp a beat of jazz for your razzamatazz that sends me

Ba Boom Click, Click, Click

Sometimes the softness of your notes makes me want to cry inside and give it a stroke. The pain I feel from the love of your touch gives me a tingle from breath, I cannot lie. Just keep playing my sax and keep slaying my jazz, it's like that. Because of the burning, sizzling sounds that will always stay around. Oh, yes, how I love that sound.

Ba Boom Click, Click, Click!!!

That's the sound of jazz coming from my lips

Dance with me, wrap me in the soul of your tapestry. The thump-thump of your drum sending my heart on a journey to which it can never overcome. That soothing sound entitles me to wear a crown! Oh, that's jazz, you keep me dancing.

Ba Boom Click, Click, Click

Now that's the sound of jazz felt from the bottom of my toes to the top of my lips, I swing my hips to the rhythm

Ba Boom Click, Click, Click

Don't stop now, you just hit that ultimate sound that can reach all over town to the underground, can you feel me? Ahhh, yeah!

Ba Boom Click, Click, Click

Now that's the sound of jazz played from my lips

SOLDIER

It's hard when ya fighting on the battlefields of life
Always looking around, searching for
Who's coming at you with a knife
Are they there for ya
or is it your life
You gotta take them down while you're wearing your crown
because you're
just a soldier
wearing your battle gear on your arms.
'cause
I'm just a soldier

On my knees is where I belong
Not standing here cursing and fighting
looking at you always backbiting.
Changing your words, knowing what I heard
coming at me, insulting my degree,
trying to stump all over me.
Hey, hey, but ya can't
because
I'm a soldier.

I know to whom I belong,
He's always in charge.
You can't bring me down.
On this I agree, because I'm a soldier.
So don't get me wrong, just back up off of me.
I'm a SOLDIER!!!

I'm standing free

Stand strong
He know where I belong
'cause I'm a soldier.

I stand up and fight, always doing what's right
never taking a life.
Only living, loving, and always giving delights.
I'm a soldier.

MARCHING ON, MARCHING, MARCHING, MARCHING

I'm strong—don't get me wrong
'cause whom am I?

I'm GOD'S

SOLDIER

REVENGEANCE

I don't know what to do, I feel like a
deer caught in headlights, unable to move
thinking this might be the night of my last life
you keep pushing and picking and thinking
you're bad and I don't know what to do
so I
just walk away and go ahead
thinking and wishing and praying that this would all end
but then you come back and punch me
with an evil grin.
You try to wear me down with those demon ways,
but you'll get nowhere
when you look to your later days.
Yeah, my pain was just for a moment in time
but you'll have yours for as long as you live
because I'll always be on your mind.

REVENGEANCE!!!!

LOVE OF LIFE

Hello! Hello!!
Pleased to meet you. This is our second chance at this
so let's not get this wrong
hold out yours and catch me in
your arms
watch me smile as I take a leap of faith.
The Heavens brought me to you, so don't make
me wait.
You say you always wanted me, now I'm here
to stay
this world is big and frightening
please show me the way.
Times are hard, I cannot lie, but as
you struggle on my life I can feel the pressure
on my life.
I know I can find comfort from loving you,
Because your life lessons shows your loving from what
you've been through.
So, I'm here and ready, just say when
open up your arms and I'll lovingly
jump in!

DOODLY DAT

Doodly Dat Doodly Dat
I have a big, fat, happy cat

He walks on air
Dances on stairs
He acts like a dog
who likes to fetch
throwing the fluffy blue ball
he likes to catch as he
doodly dat, my fat, happy cat

you can't help but smile
because that scat cat has a jazzy style
as he doodly dat
when he chats with the cutest smile

I love that!!!!
Doodly Dat Doodly Dat
I have a big, fat, happy cat.

Watch how he dances like Fred Astaire
amazing the world and makes you dare
not to stare as he marvels that cloud that he's on
where he can do no wrong
as he
Doodly Dat Doodly Dat
All Night
Long!

I MISS YOU

I miss you
The you that's part of me
The you that's the heart of me
The you that holds the card in me

I miss you
Like the river that parts the sea
I miss you

If a bird could not kiss the sky
If a bee could not sting my thigh
I miss you

You were my love that conquered all the wars
The one who would chase away all the bad
Baby, you touch my soul deep within.
I don't know what I'll do without you
All I gotta say is…
I miss you!!!!!

BECAUSE OF YOU

I am smart
I have a big heart
There is only one place it could have come from

Because of you my life is full of fun
I love to swing and dance
I have learned the art of romance
Because of you
life is never dull
and I am learning you are never too old
to dance and take a chance at life

Because of you
I know I can
There is no journey unknown to man
that I cannot do.
Who would I be if you didn't teach me to love me?
Where would I be if you didn't teach me to dream?
All because of
you!

KITTY CAT LOVE
Purr Purr Purr
Scat cat, sit down
Meow, now purr

NIGHT OF MY HEART
Oceans, moon, love
Cradles in my heart, stands
Lover man holds

CAPTIVATED
Captive over you
You've held me too
In your arms

WARS
Fight, be strong
Lay down your arms, man
Be jamming now

MUSIC FLOWS
Rock'n Soul
Riverbed flow with love
Come home, sea

SEASONS CHANGE
To summer fun
Jumping around, clowns with smiles
Turtles crawl, fall

I'M BLACK
Hands down
Please don't shoot me
I'm just like you

HONEYSUCKLES LOVE
Honeysuckles
Best friends on hills
Sisters

I AM WHO I AM

I am worthy
You try to mistreat me
I am worthy

I am beautiful
Your words cannot kill me
I am beautiful

I am wonderful
Trying to tear me down
I am wonderful

I am strong
You want to poison me
I am strong

I am loved
You are a monster
I am loved

I am disciplined
You cannot discourage me
I am disciplined

I AM WHO I AM
      And I am loved
           No one can change that

My Best Friend

We played all day until the night
We walked around and sometimes we'd fight

My best friend was strong and true;
always covering my back
and
always knew what to do

We would laugh and cry
dine and pine
but we'd always be together
me and my best friend

Too bad you're gone
the pain in my heart for you lives on
I miss you
I love you
My best friend

A TITLE, A NAME

The past to the present
Has shown to be strong
Some people in your
position showed to be right or wrong

But as for you
You have shown nothing but
how to make an
ass out of
you

You have taken the beautiful
title and made a mockery
out of the throne
to which was held high
and was known and respected
throughout the world to which was
known to everyone and
is now your home

We are now ashamed to even call
you by the title you have
questionably been given.
Shall we say your name,
all because of fame you
wanted to hold that name?

Who are you?

A TITLE, A NAME!

SISTERS
We play today
Jumping, swinging, stomping, and spinning
We all fall down

SWIM
Splash over here
Look at my soul swing
Conquer fear, dear

SOUNDS
Silence inside me
I can't hear a thing pounding
Car horns loud

LISTEN
Pluck Pluck Pluck
Oceans, moon, rivers flow, streams
Dance one way

THE SOUNDS
Music I see
Do Dat Do Dat Woo
Look at me

WHO
Moon, sun, fog
Spiritual, wonderful, loved, creative, adored
Tomorrow, today, yesterday

CHANGES
Step soft slow
Sea crashes on the shore
I see fire

WHO ARE WE?
Alone hermit privacy
Cat lady, lover, bitchie players
Vagabond, lonely dreamers

OOOOH! I LIKE IT
Shack it up
Lake is overflowing, lover
Boogie down now

TURN OFF THE LIGHTS

Don't open my doors
or
try looking in my eyes
because sometimes you call
you'll get a surprise
it's dark in there, baby, I swear
someone has dampened my heart
I thought I was strong
until a sinkhole ripped us apart

no, no, baby
turn off the lights
my eyes are so red
my room is cluttered, you can no longer see my bed

For as cluttered as the mind is
as dampened my soul
such as life to it my world has gone cold.
Baby, turn off the lights
what's old is not new.
My head shall be covered and my heart will be too.

Turn off the lights
Can you hear my cries?
Or are you ignoring the truth that lies inside?
The trees are calling
but there is no answer
because I ask for you to please just turn
off the lights and let me be

Just turn off the lights!

There's no future for you and me
No need for me to explain
no more begging, my tears are enough, it's insane
turn off the lights and walk out that door
time is up, I can't see you anymore

I turned off the lights to our relationship
to open the door for a path so clear
one that shows me that I don't need you, dear,
so I'll turn off the lights!

My Butterfly

What is this sound I hear?
Is it because I lost my butterfly? This sound is haunting, it scares my soul with its deepened moans, I quiver its gesture of terror. When! When will it stop? Misplaced emotions won't part me, I shiver in their wake. While the river streams down my face. How can that one sound render so much pain? The moans, the rainfall, was it worth it all due to the loss of my butterfly?

The wailing sounds so high, I cannot bear the sounds. Like the wind blowing, knocking at my door.

Tap! Tap! Tap! Tap on my floor is sounds of my teardrops. Come back to me, my butterfly, please, it's so dark in here. This deafening sound is heavy like a heartbeat.

Making me wondering about my life and what it could be.

Instead I'll close my eyes and look ahead, my butterfly will always be there. I'll hold my breath and keep my eyes closed, praying for my butterfly.

SEE MY BODY

Full hips, tender lips, that's the way you see my body
but I'm just not satisfied
because you can structure it like buying
clothing from the rack just because I don't like my back

Just looking at my full hips, shrinking lips
I want a pucker that will send a sucker
mad with passionate dreamlike
I'm his starlet, not some lima bean

I don't have those full hip, big tits
the way you see my body.
My breasts are sagging at best,
I want on a lift and tuck, so who gives
a fuck about that!

But nature call was at the mall of
my selection. I flip a page and
dial that name and give it all
away just to fit the mold of others
so who cares about my mother's nature
design that they say was fine
we are talking about my body, soul, and mind.

Just look at my flat behind
when you talk about my full hips, big tits, tender lips,
tiny waist disgrace. It's all in how I see myself.

I gotta love me?
Because of what you think of me

My life hurts—that's why I cut myself to renew
myself just so you'll love me.
I'll take a nip tuck to my butt, so what
see my body, I wanna be your hottie

My loved ones say no, that's not the way to go,
I'm taking my history. But it's no mystery
not a history lesson that I need for me.
I just need the blessing.

The blessing of that blade to my thick thighs
that will fix them just right and that will make
me look like heaven. Do you feel me?

I look to love myself, know myself
'cause that's the way you see my body and its imperfections.
My full lips, tight waist ...

SEE MY BODY

JUST RELAX

Come on in
I know you're tired
After all, you've had a hard day at work
here, let me help you out of those clothes and into the shower
I'll step inside and be that one desire
here, let me lend a hand, you missed a
spot where that drip didn't drop

I want to kiss you here and there while
the room steams up everywhere
it's time to come out but don't you dare
dry off, I have something waiting for you in there
In the other room
Come go with me so I can make your
body swoon to the beat of relaxation from frustration.

My candles are lit with loving care, my oil is warm
just right for your body, baby, I just wanted you to be aware.
Now lay across my bed, please,
I want to rub your body down with that oil, baby, too easy
every part of you that needs my love
I won't skip a part because I'm starting from the top
from front to back, only if we can make it like that
"Mmmm!" was that a moan I heard
"Mmmm!" Do it again, baby, you like that?
Let's make it a third, your body so warm
I must treat it with care, now just relax—shhh! We're almost there and
just know I love you and really I just wanted you to

Go to bed, goodnight!

QUESTIONABLE

My history, your history
Is forever changing
she arrived on a pedestal
with chains around her feet
but told to be sent back
because we can't show
her mystique

We hide our shame of truth of abuse
but show the glory of a lie that's used
to show an image of how one man is
free
and another is a slave
never
to give way to the real way of life of
how we are today.
So we hide the truth with our statues of truth of lies.

Please come to us, you are welcomed
here
only if you are one way and not another,
the one we fear.
Yes, we are proud
we hold our heads up high
but
we will deny all of the backstabbing
dehumanizing by saying bring me your
huddled masses and yet we'll kick
you out and kept some giving them backlashes

Don't search for my torch of flame
because if you turn your back you might get blamed
for something you did not do, so my sisters and brothers
look ahead of you, this is no game

I'm sorry to say
but just look around these days
sometimes home is not where you want to be today

Sure, send us your poor
so we can close the door
why not, we already have a tiny island we ignore

We have people in power stepping up with big fat lies
who want to jeopardize us and send us back in time
where they have dreams of delusions
to keep down other races and deal with a lot of collusions
I don't know about our days and time
with the way things are, they leave a lot heavy on the mind
it might even leave it
Questionable!

THANK YOU

I woke up to the sunshine
no clouds in the sky
there was no reason to cry
only reasons to try
I just wanna, Thank You
Thank You
Thank You
Say it loud Say it now

As in life we're going to hit some bumpy roads
have no place to go
have no one to hold
crying on the phone
getting an eviction note
losing all hope

But I just turn around and I see
it's not always going to be that way
no, it won't

It's just one of those rainy days
but I just wanna say Thank You
Thank You
Thank You, Lord

I feel your hand upon my life, I never have to turn around and ask twice
because I know you're here for me, I've gotten down on my knees,
asking you
please and knowing now you've blessed me with ease.
I've just gotta! I've just gotta Thank You, Lord

Thank You
Thank You

There were times when I've been close to death,
times when I've been drowning in debt
and there was no one I could turn to
but who has been there for me but you

Thank you for the sun
Thank you for the rain

I know that sometimes in life there will be pain
I just wanna say thank you anyway
Look at all of the birds and how they fly away,
look at how you love no matter
what we do that day
thank you
Thank You!

I just gotta, I just gotta
Thank You
Thank You

SHALL WE DANCE

You and I hand in hand under the moonlit sky
guided by romance
my heart is warm, beating with yours
as our feet are bare on the floor
as I said it was you to whom I adore
     shall we dance

With your hand in mine I knew all of the
time you'd be mine forever to grind
     shall we dance

Never letting go
you oughtta know how much I loved
your kisses so hot, they hit that dot
no man has ever been able to find
please
     shall we dance

TOUCHING ME

Touching me
Touching me
Touching me

My body is not yours
So try to understand that
Don't just touch and grab all over me
It'll come with a fee
when you're locked up and they
throw away the key
all because you touched what was not
yours

Touching me
Touching me
Touching me

I love my body
adore who I am, you come along and try to strip that again
people say it's my fault if I don't report the assault until some years later
or they just call me an instigator

Don't touch me
you don't own me
this is my body
not just anybody can have my body
no matter my occupation
no matter the situation
my body belongs to me

Touching me
Touching me
Touching me

No can do
it may leave you black and blue

Touching me
Touching me
Touching me

Don't call me asking me to go down South
in any direction
that's just out
I'm beating my chest
that's just out

TOUCHING ME,

DON'T!!!!!!

MY WORTH

What's my worth? That's a question that I shouldn't have been given since birth. When I was born I was swaddled in love. As I got older time chipped away from me with its hand and its glove.

People tried to pull me down just because I gained or picked up a pimple or two. Hey, but it's puberty, so what am I to do?

Then they looked at my complexion, saying it's not sheer perfection Claiming I'm not a perfect 10, laughing and pointing, making me question my friends.

You send out messages on the internet, telling people how I'm not at my best. Trying to bully me and sometimes I'm not a child. I can be an adult and they can do it office style.

Look, just because you have issues of you own, don't try and tear me down and make your Christmas wish of being better than me. All because you see in me what you ought to be.

Yes, I'm beautiful, big, intelligent, bold, and strong. Strong willed and strong minded, just 'cause you can't find it don't take me with you and try to make me unglued. I arrive with a smile and sport my own style.

Soooooo!!!! Guess what, I do remember and know my worth. You nor anyone else define me. I am the me I am supposed to be. Remember this my worth is NOT YOURS!!!!!!!!!!

I Want to Take a Journey with You

I want to take a journey with you
the sky is so blue
it makes me fall more in love with you
no one seems to understand you
nor can reach the core that holds you
let's kiss the sky
and ride on that cloud, then ride it to a
journey that no man can deny

I want to take a journey with you

You have reached a part of me that no man
has ever seen
ever known
could ever make me their home
as we spread those wings
we can learn almost everything
only if you'll let us be

Stop, don't fight the wind
you'll never know of how many or how much
true love you can let in
don't hold me down
let's say it with a smile

There are creatures below who want to see
us grow
so I just wanted you to know
I want to take a journey with you

Have no fear
in life the wind can be rough and strong
but eventually
it can slow and be calm
and we can be fiercely

I want to take a journey with you
to see how you change
how you grow
to see how you love
and how much you know

I want to take a journey with you
as we grow old
I would love to see your grace
the way you nurture
brings a smile to my face
as time sets in our wings, spread thine
hold strong, my friend, know my love
is always with you
forever within
and no end

Thank you for the journey

LEVEL

Tomorrow never shines as bright as yesterday
Today you may not feel as young as last you felt weak
But right now you sparkle as like a diamond that would never die for a lifetime and no one can take that away

Just as a child goes from preschool to college, you obtain knowledge and never allow anyone to tear you down. So, why now do you stand here crying, saying someone saying bad things about you, trying to bring you down? Just remember your name and know you the levels from which you came, and I promise that that person(s) won't be but a stain. A stain in life never to be able to reach your level of fame.

No, you're not a movie star nor on the pop charts, but you are famous on another level to which no one could ever be, which is you. FABULOUS YOU!

Everyone has their own fame levels in life, which one is yours?

Think twice?

FABULOUS YOU! Which is twice as nice.

I'm in Love with a Bad Boy

Hip-hopping, lip-locking, crack-rocking
Baby, you really turn me on
the facts right, he can get all night
with that body so tight he can get it, all right
baby, you're all that I want

I just love the bad boy with all of his corny lines
coming at me with those lame story times
body so hot I can bounce dime, a dollar, fifty dollars
or maybe one hundred off his chest, which is best or even easy to lay
upon because
I just wanna put my head on his chest to keep me safe and warm when I
can't rest

Sometimes his rhymes are so def
and make me shake my booty to death
I lose my mind with without control
listening to my baby playing his music so loud
it reaches my soul

    Oh, I'm in love with a bad boy

My man so good he can use my body for his toy
fast girls, fast cars, that's what they think are the joys of
bussing caps, playing with guns, deep down they're just
sweet honey buns

    I'm in love with a bad boy

Talking smack, chitchat just for fun, now it's begun:

"You playing? I playing, don't even think about it!"
He raised his hand (smiling), he still my man

      I'm in love with a bad boy

You got me standing by your side in the middle of the night
holding your stash while you're making some cash

'Cause I'm in love with a bad boy
Car drive-by taking our lives, I know I'm with you and my love is true

Thump Thump   Thump   Beeeeep

     Flatline, we're in the
       morgue

As we cross into the great beyond you grab my hand and FINALLY say:
"I love you, you're my ride-or-die chick."
I say, "Boy, get the fuck out of here, it's a little too late, had I known who I was then I would have had another date."
     PEACE!!!
       I thought I was in love with a bad boy!

TODAY IS JUST LIKE YESTERDAY

Sitting at a bus stop looking
really fresh and hot
you slide up to me, calling me a cutie
all because we don't look, the same people wanna
call us a name back from the day and age of the slavery era

You mean I can't love who
I want to love like Mr. and Mrs. Loving from Virginia
Whatever!!!
What does race have to do with it?
All I see is love that was sent to me from Heaven above

Today is just like yesterday!

I want a good education but you wanna
feed me misinformation fed by your administration
all you are causing is more frustration
I mean, I know what my brother Mr. Martin Luther King
marched for and my grandmothers
protesting and beating down your door for,
they were looking for a better day
You just can't take that away through their knowledge
I mean, what the heck, for the more I step
forth the more you wanna step back

Man, today is just like yesterday!

Yes, you might not be hiding under any
form of coverup, but the way you're treating
people today sure seems just messed up

When are we just going to love one another
help one another and know that we are just like one another
heck, we are just sisters and brothers
on this big planet born to love
Please put an end to this tragic way of life called hate and shame
So we can no longer make a mistake of living a lie and killing our future

Today is just like yesterday

No More!!

IT'S GOING TO BE ALL RIGHT

I remember when I used to skin my knee
cry and say I can't see
all because my tears were so intense
you would be right there for me
saying it would be all right

After your long day at work I would wrap
myself around you no matter how much
you hurt, but you would say
everything is all right

You would take me on trips and teach me
new tricks and laugh when I was not
funny and say that's all right, honey, it's going to be all right

You were my protector
my corrector
my under-the-bed inspector
my Superman
always giving me a hand
saying it's going to be all right
thank you, Daddy!!!
I love you, as we grew up you became best
pals, thank you

You walked with me
talked with me
held my hands
you told me everything will be all right
you gave me my first dance

you thought me to fight
how to fly a kite
kissed me goodnight

I love you, Daddy, I grew up with you
you got me through my life
showing me and teaching me that everything is going to be all right

VISITORS

Thank you for your time
you were so sweet, gentle, and kind
you touched my heart with such loving care
though you were here but a moment
our time felt like as it was an eternity
thank you for being a part of me
a visitor
who came to
see me

HATE ME

Why do you hate me? You don't even know me
when I bleed don't I bleed just like you
when I cry aren't our tears just the same

Why are you so hard on me
what did I do to you
all I do is exist
now you put a handcuff on my wrist, spit on me,
and sometimes you defame my name
all because I yearn to be free like you,
now what can I do

I was told your country was the free,
the brave and was built on those who were
from other countries, no one person was the same

Look, one day you're gonna need me, I can create something to save you
to enhance your life and propel you

Don't overlook me, I could be you or related,
look down your history line and see

You may start hating what you're doing to me and others, just look in the
mirror, you'll see, then your heart will be in pain from all of the misery
that you have put us through, you can change it

It's up to you! Please stop hating me....
Know me, love me! Because I'm you!!!!

Why do you hate me, is it because we don't look the same
or because we call our religion by another name?
Look, just because my skin is different from yours
doesn't mean I won't matter to you, with the way they are swapping
around organs today you may be in need of mine one day
or my blood is something you're strutting around with today

So before you keep looking at me with hate, know we are all the same,
our bodies work the same, please stop hating because of my name
STOP HATE!!!!!

www.ingramcontent.com/pod-product-compliance
Lightning Source LLC
Chambersburg PA
CBHW020337010526
44119CB00001B/20